DALLAS
Mavericks

BY ELLEN LABRECQUE

Published by The Child's World®
1980 Lookout Drive • Mankato, MN 56003-1705
800-599-READ • www.childsworld.com

Acknowledgments
The Child's World®: Mary Berendes, Publishing Director
Red Line Editorial: Editorial direction
The Design Lab: Design
Amnet: Production

Design elements: PhotoDisc, Viorika Prikhodko/
iStockphoto

Photographs ©: Bret Hartman/AP Images, cover, title;
Tony Gutierrez/AP Images, 5, 6, 21; Reed Saxon/AP
Images, 9; Mike Fuentes/AP Images, 10; The Dallas
Morning News/Louis DeLuca/AP Images, 13; Tom
DiPace/AP Images, 17; David Phillip/AP Images, 18; AP
Images, 22; Nick Wass/AP Images, 25; John F. Rhodes/
AP Images, 26

ISBN 978-1623234997
LCCN 2013931334

Printed in the United States of America
Mankato, MN
July, 2013
PA02171

About the Author

Ellen Labrecque has written books for young readers on basketball, tennis, ice hockey, and other sports. Ellen used to work for *Sports Illustrated Kids* magazine and has written about many NBA stars. She likes to watch basketball. The Philadelphia 76ers are her favorite team.

Table *of* Contents

Go, Mavericks!

The Dallas Mavericks play in Texas. It is known as the "Lone Star State." The Mavericks also have a team filled with stars! Their fans expect the team to play fast and furious basketball and also to have a lot of fun. Are the Mavericks your favorite team? Let's meet the Dallas Mavericks!

The Dallas Mavericks give their fans a lot to cheer about!

Who Are the Mavericks?

The Dallas Mavericks play in the National Basketball Association (NBA). The Mavericks are sometimes called the "Mavs" for short. They are one of 30 teams in the NBA. The NBA includes the Eastern Conference and the Western Conference. The Mavericks play in the Southwest Division of the Western Conference. The Eastern Conference champion plays the Western Conference champion in the **NBA Finals**. The Mavericks have played in the NBA Finals twice. They won for the first time in 2011.

The Mavericks' O. J. Mayo goes up for an easy basket.

Where They Came From

The Dallas team joined the NBA in 1980. At first, nobody knew what to name the team. A local radio station had a "Name the Team" contest. The final choices came down to the Mavericks, the Wranglers, and the Express. The name Mavericks won out. A maverick is someone who does things differently from many other people. The current Mavs are actually the second pro basketball team to play in Dallas. The Dallas Chaparrals played in the American Basketball Association (ABA) from 1967 to 1973. They moved to San Antonio. Today, that team is called the Spurs.

The Mavericks faced off against the great Earvin "Magic" Johnson (in yellow) and the Los Angeles Lakers in the 1984 playoffs.

Who They Play

The Mavericks play 82 games each season. That's a lot of basketball! They play every other NBA team at least once each season. They play teams in their division and conference more often. The San Antonio Spurs and the Houston Rockets are the Mavs' two biggest **rivals**. These three teams play in the same division and the same state. Combined, this "Texas Triangle" has played in 10 NBA Finals. The Mavs made the championship series for the first time in 2006.

Dallas takes on San Antonio in a battle from the "Texas Triangle."

Where They Play

Dallas players live and play in style. The American Airlines Center is the Mavericks' home. The arena and the locker rooms are some of the nicest in the NBA. Every player's locker has a flat-screen TV, a DVD player, and a video-game machine! The players also have their own lounge. It includes a pool table and a giant TV. Inside the arena, bench players sit on chairs with comfy cushions. After every game, both teams are offered a giant buffet of food.

A Mavericks fan cheers outside American Airlines Center in Dallas.

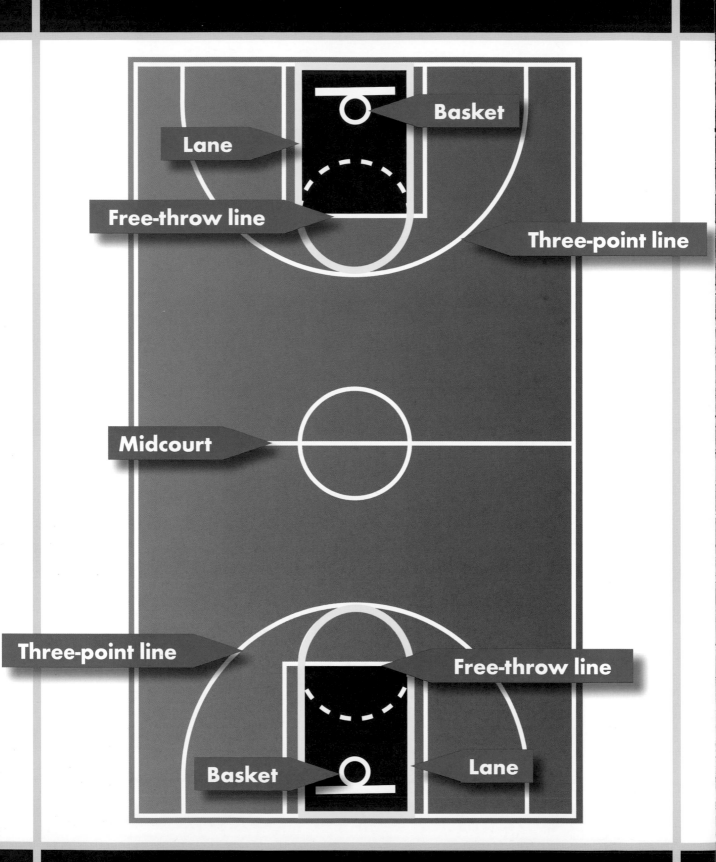

Basket

Lane

Free-throw line

Three-point line

Midcourt

Three-point line

Free-throw line

Basket

Lane

The Basketball Court

Basketball is played on a court made of wood. An NBA court is 94 feet (29 m) long. A painted line shows the middle of the court. Other lines lay out the free-throw area. The space below each basket is known as the "lane." The baskets at each end are 10 feet (3 meters) off the ground. The metal rims of the baskets stick out over the court. Nylon nets hang from the rims.

Big Days

The Dallas Mavericks have had many great moments in their history. Here are three of the greatest:

1984: The Mavs made the **playoffs** for the first time. Then they beat the Seattle SuperSonics to advance to the second round.

2006: The Mavs made it to the NBA Finals for the first time. However, they fell to the Miami Heat, 4–2.

2011: Dallas reached the NBA Finals for the second time. It was a rematch of the 2006 championship series. This time the Mavericks beat the Heat in six games!

Dirk Nowitzki and the Mavericks celebrate with the NBA championship trophy in 2011.

Tough Days

The Mavericks can't win all their games. Some games or seasons don't turn out well. The players keep trying to play their best, though. Here are some of the toughest seasons in Mavericks history:

1993: Dallas finished the season with just 11 wins. Its 11–71 record was the second worst in NBA history.

2000: The Mavs missed the playoffs for the tenth straight time. However, a streak of 10-plus playoff appearances began the next season.

2007: The Mavericks won a team-record 67 games in the regular season. However, they lost to the Golden State Warriors in the first round of the playoffs.

Many teams had their way with the Mavericks in 1992–93.

Meet the Fans

Dallas fans love their hoops. But they also support their troops. In 2004, the team started a tradition. The Mavericks wanted to pay tribute to the U.S. troops. So fans donated their front-row seats to injured soldiers. The "Seats for Soldiers" tradition continued in 2012. At the game, the soldiers receive loud cheers from the crowd. They get cheers from the Dallas players, too!

Mavs Man stands with U.S. soldiers for the national anthem at "Seats for Soldiers" night in Dallas.

Heroes Then . . .

The Mavericks have had some great players.
Guards Brad Davis and Rolando Blackman played
together for 11 seasons mostly in the 1980s. They
are the only two Mavs to have their numbers retired.
That means no other Dallas players will wear their
jersey numbers. **Point guard** Jason Kidd was one
of the best. He could do many things very well. Kidd
began his career in Dallas from 1994 to 1996. He
came back to Dallas in 2008. Kidd helped the team
win the 2011 NBA title. **Swingman** Michael Finley
was another Mavericks star. He was a great shooter.

Brad Davis used his great dribbling skills to get past defenders.

Heroes Now . . .

Dirk Nowitzki is the best-known Mavericks player. He is one of the best 7-foot-tall players ever. The big man from Germany shoots a **fadeaway jumper** that is hard to defend. In 2007, Nowitzki was named the NBA's Most Valuable Player (MVP). He was also the 2011 NBA Finals MVP. **Forward** Shawn Marion was also on that championship team. He is one of the NBA's great all-around players.

Dirk Nowitzki became the Mavericks' first NBA MVP in 2007.

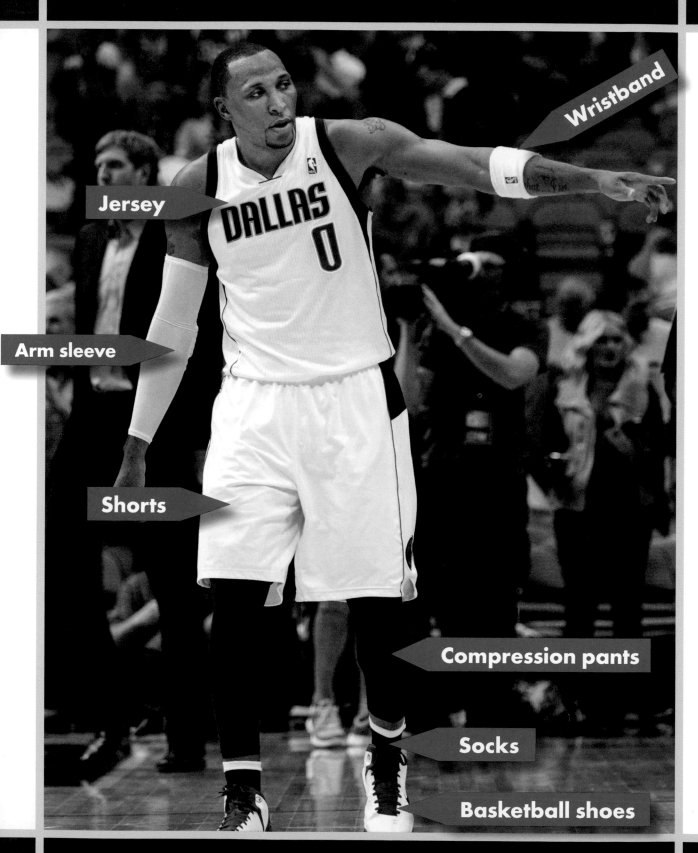

Wristband

Jersey

Arm sleeve

Shorts

Compression pants

Socks

Basketball shoes

Gearing Up

Dallas Mavericks players wear the team's uniform and special basketball sneakers. Some wear other pads to protect themselves. Check out this picture of Shawn Marion and learn about what NBA players wear.

THE BASKETBALL

NBA basketballs are made of leather. Several pieces are held together with rubber edges. Inside the leather ball is a hollow ball of rubber. This is filled with air. The leather is covered with little bumps called "pebbles." The pebbles help players get a good grip on the ball. The basketball used in the Women's National Basketball Association (WNBA) is slightly smaller than the men's basketball.

Shawn Marion wears lots of accessories during games.

Note: All numbers shown are through the 2012–13 season.

HIGH SCORERS

These players have scored the most points for the Mavericks.

PLAYER	POINTS
Dirk Nowitzki	25,051
Rolando Blackman	16,643

HELPING HAND

Here are Dallas' all-time leaders in **assists**.

PLAYER	ASSISTS
Derek Harper	5,111
Brad Davis	4,524

CLEANING THE BOARDS

Rebounds are a big part of the game. Here are the Mavericks' best rebounders.

PLAYER	REBOUNDS
Dirk Nowitzki	9,096
James Donaldson	4,589

MOST THREE-POINT SHOTS MADE

Shots taken from behind a line about 23 feet (7 m) from the basket are worth three points. Here are the Mavericks' best at these long-distance shots.

PLAYER	THREE-POINT BASKETS
Dirk Nowitzki	1,340
Jason Terry	1,140

COACH

Who coached the Mavericks to the most wins?

Don Nelson, 339

assists passes to teammates that lead directly to making baskets

fadeaway jumper a shot that a player takes while jumping away from the basket

forward one of two tall players who rebound and score near the basket

guards two players who set up plays, pass to teammates closer to the basket, and shoot from farther away

NBA Finals the seven-game NBA championship series, in which the champion must win four games

playoffs a series of games between 16 teams that decides which two teams will play in the NBA Finals

point guard the team's main ball handler who brings the ball up the court and sets up the offense

rebounds missed shots that bounce off the backboard or rim and are grabbed by another player

rivals teams that play each other often and have an ongoing competition

swingman a player who can play both forward and guard

FIND OUT MORE

BOOKS

Hareas, John. *Championship Teams*. New York: Scholastic, 2010.

Ladewski, Paul. *Megastars*. New York: Scholastic, 2011.

Ladewski, Paul. *NBA: Hoop Heroes.* New York: Scholastic, 2009.

Osier, Dan. *Dirk Nowitzki*. New York: PowerKids Press, 2011.

Smallwood, John N. *Megastars*. New York: Scholastic, 2011.

WEB SITES

Visit our Web site for links about the Dallas Mavericks and other NBA teams:
childsworld.com/links

Note to Parents, Teachers, and Librarians: We routinely verify our Web links to make sure they are safe and active sites. So encourage your readers to check them out!

INDEX